Manners at School

by Carrie Finn   illustrated by Chris Lensch

PICTURE WINDOW BOOKS
Minneapolis, Minnesota

Special thanks to our advisers for their expertise:

Kay Augustine, Associate Director
Institute for Character Development at Drake University

Susan Kesselring, M.A., Literacy Educator
Rosemount–Apple Valley–Eagan (Minnesota) School District

Editor: Nick Healy
Designer: Tracy Davies
Page Production: Brandie Shoemaker
Art Director: Nathan Gassman
Associate Managing Editor: Christianne Jones
The illustrations in this book were created digitally.

Picture Window Books
1710 Roe Crest Drive
North Mankato, MN 56003
www.capstonepub.com

Printed in the United States of America in North Mankato, Minnesota.
012012   006552R

 All books published by Picture Window Books
are manufactured with paper containing at least
10 percent post-consumer waste.

Library of Congress Cataloging-in-Publication Data
Finn, Carrie.
Manners at school / by Carrie Finn ; illustrated by
Chris Lensch.
p. cm. – (Way to be!)
Includes bibliographical references and index.
ISBN-13: 978-1-4048-3151-3 (library binding)
ISBN-13: 978-1-4048-3551-1 (paperback)
1. Etiquette for children and teenagers. I. Lensch, Chris. II. Title.
BJ1857.C5F47 2007
395.5–dc22   2006027303

Your school is a busy place. Using good manners can make it nicer for everyone. Good manners can also help everyone learn. Good manners show respect for teachers and classmates.

There are lots of ways you can use good manners at school.

Olivia gets to class on time each day. She always says, "Good morning, Miss Martin."

She is using good manners.

Arnold gives his full attention to his teacher's directions.

He is using good manners.

seed

water

light

When her teacher asks the class to be quiet during a movie, Madeline stops talking to her friends.

She is using good manners.

Paul keeps his eyes on his own work. He never peeks at his neighbor's paper.

He is using good manners.

Alan and Cory stand in line quietly before recess.

They are using good manners.

Jamie cleans up her table after art class.

She is using good manners.

Owen raises his hand
to ask his teacher
a question.

He is using good manners.

Dot shares her colored pencils
with Alexandra.

She is using good manners.

Marco finishes his math test before his classmates do. He asks the teacher if he may borrow a book during his free time.

He is using good manners.

It's important to use good manners whenever you are in class. Good manners keep the classroom running smoothly.

Fun Facts

In Haiti, kids talk to their teachers only when asked a question.

In Russia, people celebrate the Day of Knowledge on the first day of each school year.

In Australia, children begin the school year in February and finish in December.

In Japan, students clean the school at the end of each day.

In France, most children start going to school when they are 3 years old.

Teachers were once paid with food or a place to live. That's why students still give their teachers apples.

To Learn More

More Books to Read

Candell, Arianna. *Mind Your Manners: In School*. Hauppauge, N.Y.: Barron's, 2005.

DeGezelle, Terri. *Manners in the Classroom*. Mankato, Minn.: Capstone Press, 2004.

Thomas, Pat. *My Manners Matter: A First Look at Being Polite*. Hauppauge, N.Y.: Barron's, 2006.

On the Web

FactHound offers a safe, fun way to find Web sites related to topics in this book.

All of the sites on FactHound have been researched by our staff.

1. Visit *www.facthound.com*

2. Type in this special code: 1404831517

3. Click on the FETCH IT button.

Your trusty FactHound will fetch the best sites for you!

Index

Look for all of the books in the Way to Be! series: